The Best Keto Side-Dish 2021

Healthy Keto side dishes

Sommario

INTRODUCTION

Congratulations on being here.

In this book we will talk about side dishes, a fundamental dish to accompany a great meal.

Perfect to accompany meat or fish dishes, or even simply to be enjoyed alone.

Side dishes are among the best dishes in the keto diet, they accompany the main dishes and give us a great dose of protein by promoting ketosis.

I have enclosed in this book my favorite side dishes, in a simple way to be prepared by everyone.

Let's start cooking right away

SIDE DISH RECIPES

OVEN-BAKED RUTABAGA WEDGES

Ingredients

- 1 lb rutabaga

- ¼ cup olive oil

- 1 tsp chili powder or paprika powder

- salt and pepper

Instructions

9. Preheat the oven to 200 ° C temperature.

10. Rinse the rutabagas and peel them. Smaller roots in the oven are going to bake quicker.

11. Break into wedges and spread over a sheet of baking.

12. Salt and potatoes. Sprinkle on top of olive oil and blend well.

13. Place in the oven and bake for 20 min.

Macros: Net Carbs 18 % (7 g) Fiber 3 g Fat 79 % (14 g) Protein 3 % (1 g) 167

Prep time:25 min; **Servings:** 4

CREAMY LEMON GREEN BEANS

Ingredients

- 10 oz fresh green beans

- 3 oz butter or olive oil

- ½ tsp sea salt

- ¼ tsp ground black pepper

- 1 cup heavy whipping cream

- ½ lemon, the zest

- ½ cup fresh parsley (optional)

Instructions

1. Trim the green beans and rinse them.

2. In a pan, heat butter or oil.

3. Sauté the beans over medium-high heat for 3-4 min until they start to brown. Reduce the temperature to the maximum— to taste salt and pepper.

4. Remove heavy cream and cook for 1-2 min Apply the lemon zest thinly and sprinkle before serving on the green beans.

5. Until serving, add the finely chopped parsley.

Macros: Net Carbs 5 % (5 g) Fiber 2 g Fat 91 % (39 g) Protein 3 % (3 g) 376

Prep time: 25 min; **Servings:** 4

CAPRESE SNACK

Ingredients

9. 8 oz cherry tomatoes

10. 8 oz mozzarella, mini cheese balls

11. 2 Tbsp green pesto

12. salt and pepper

Instructions

4. Split into half the vegetables and nuts of mozzarella. Remove and blend the pesto.

5. To taste salt and pepper.

Macros: Net Carbs 6 % (3 g) Fiber 1 g Fat 69 % (17 g) Protein 25 % (14 g) 218

Prep time: 5 min; **Servings:** 4

KETO EGGPLANT HASH WITH EGGS

Ingredients

- 1 yellow onion, finely chopped

- 2 Tbsp olive oil

- ½ lb halloumi cheese, diced into small cubes

- 2 eggplants, diced

- salt and pepper

- 4 eggs

- 2 Tbsp butter

- ½ tsp Worcestershire sauce (optional)

Instructions

1. In medium heat, fry the onion in the oil until soft.

2. Add eggplant and halloumi cheese and fry until all is dark golden — salt and pepper to taste.

3. Fry the eggs in a different pan as you like them and serve with a few drops of Worcestershire sauce (optional).

Prep time:20 min; **Servings:** 4

Macros: Net Carbs 11 % (11 g) Fiber 8 g Fat 69 % (31 g) Protein 20 % (20 g) 425

BRUSSELS SPROUTS WITH CARAMELIZED RED ONIONS

Ingredients

- 1 red onion

- 4 oz butter

- 1 Tbsp red wine vinegar

- salt and pepper

- 1 lb Brussels sprouts

Instructions

6. Divide the onions into wedges and fry for 5–10 min in half of the butter over medium heat.

7. The onions are supposed to turn golden but not burnt. Apply to taste the vinegar, salt, and pepper.

8. Lower the heat, when stirring, and start to sauté the onion. Place yourself on a plate.

9. Sprouts the Brussels rinse and trim and cut them in half. You can fry them all if they're tiny.

10. Fry, the Brussels sprouts with more butter in the same frying pan until a beautiful color and a little soft, has been transformed. Search with a knife or a stick. "Al dente" is best served to them.

11. Salt and potatoes. Remove and mix the onions.

Prep time: 30min; **Servings:** 4

Macros: Net Carbs 12 % (8 g) Fiber 5 g Fat 81 % (23 g) Protein 7 % (4 g) 261

KETO STUFFED MUSHROOMS

Ingredients

- 8 oz bacon

- 12 mushrooms

- 2 Tbsp butter, 3 Tbsp fresh chives, finely chopped, 1 tsp paprika powder

- 7 oz cream cheese

- salt and pepper

Instructions

- Preheat oven to 200 ° C.

- Fry the bacon until crispy. Let cool and crumble. Save the meat from the bacon.

- Cut the stems of the mushroom and finely chop. In the bacon fat, add butter if necessary.

- In a greased baking dish, put the mushrooms.

- Mix the crumbled bacon in a bowl with the fried, chopped stems of the mushroom and the other ingredients. Add to each mushroom some of the mixes.

- Bake until the mushrooms turn golden brown for 20 min

Prep time:40 min; **Servings:** 4

Macros: Net Carbs 4 % (5 g) Fiber 1 g Fat 86 % (46 g) Protein 10 % (12 g) 477

KETO BROCCOLI MASH

Ingredients

4. 1½ lbs of broccoli

5. 4 Tbsp fresh basil or fresh parsley, finely chopped

6. 3 oz butter

7. 1 garlic clove

8. salt and pepper

Instructions

1. Cut the broccoli into florets.

2. Boil the broccoli for a couple of min in plenty of lightly salted water–just enough to retain a firm texture.

3. Mix in a food processor with the other ingredients or use an immersion blender.

Prep time:15 min; **Servings:** 4

Macros: Net Carbs 14 % (7 g) Fiber 4 g Fat 76 % (18 g) Protein 10 % (5 g) 210

RUTABAGA CURLS

Ingredients

- 1½ lbs rutabaga

- 1/3 cup olive oil

- 1 Tbsp paprika powder or chili powder

- 1 tsp salt

Instructions

9. Heat the oven to 225° C (450° F). Peel and slice the rutabaga into bits you can pass through your spiralizer. Cut the long spirals to make the curls bite-sized.

10. Pour the remaining ingredients into a bowl and vigorously stir.

11. Place on a baking sheet and bake 10 min in the oven.

Prep time: 30min; **Servings:** 4

Macros: Net Carbs 20 % (11 g) Fiber 5 g Fat 76 % (18 g) Protein 4 % (2 g) 227

THAI CURRY CABBAGE

Ingredients

- 3 Tbsp coconut oil

- 1 Tbsp red curry paste preferably Thai

- 2 lbs shredded green cabbage

- 1 tsp salt

- 1 Tbsp sesame oil

Instructions

- Heat the coconut oil over high heat in a frying pan. Add curry paste and whisk for a minute. Add the cabbage.

- Saute until the cabbage starts turning golden brown

- Add 1–2 min of sesame oil and sauté

Prep time: 30 min; **Servings:** 4

Macros: Net Carbs 19 % (8 g) Fiber 6 g Fat 73 % (14 g) Protein 8 % (3 g) 181

KETO ZUCCHINI AND WALNUT SALAD

Ingredients

Dressing:

- 2 Tbsp olive oil, 3/4cup mayonnaise or vegan mayonnaise

- 2 tsp lemon juice, 1 garlic clove, finely minced

- ½ tsp salt, ¼ tsp chili powder

Salad:

- 1 head of Romaine lettuce

- 4 oz arugula lettuce ¼ cup finely chopped fresh chives or scallions

- 2 zucchini, 1 Tbsp olive oil

- Salt and pepper, 3½ oz chopped walnuts or pecans

Instructions

1. Mix the ingredients in a small dressing pan.

2. Cut the salad and cut it. Place the Romaine in a large bowl with arugula and chives.

3. Lengthwise break the zucchini and pick out the seeds. Cut half of the zucchini in quarter-inch sections.

4. In a frying pan, flame olive oil over medium heat until shimmering. Add the zucchini to the container and use salt and pepper to season. Fry until lightly browned, but solid.

5. In the salad, add cooked zucchini and blend.

6. In the same pan as the zucchini, roast the nuts briefly. Coat on a salad with salt and pepper spoon nuts and chop with salad dressing.

Prep time: 35 min; **Servings:** 4

Macros: Net Carbs 6 % (8 g) Fiber 7 g Fat 88 % (58 g) Protein 6 % (9 g) 595

KETO CAULIFLOWER CHEESE

Ingredients

- 1 lb oFrozen or fresh broccoli, cut into florets

- 1 cup heavy whipping cream

- 2 oz butter

- 7 oz cream cheese

- salt and pepper

- 2 tsp garlic powder

- 1¾ lbs cauliflower, cut into small florets

- 8 oz shredded cheese

Instructions

1. Preheat the oven to 180° C (350° F).

2. Place chopped broccoli in a bowl. Add water and bring to a boil until fork-tender .

3. When finished, strain the broccoli and discard the water, add the cream cheese, heavy whipping cream, butter, salt, pepper, and garlic powder with an immersion blender to the pot and puree. Remove the broccoli and puree together until smooth.

4. Grease a 9x12 baking dish. Place florets of cauliflower in baking dish.

5. Cover with shredded cheese and broccoli cream sauce. Bake 40 min.

Prep time: 15 min; **Servings:** 6

Macros: Net Carbs 9 % (11 g) Fiber 5 g Fat 78 % (44 g) Protein 13 % (17 g) 511

TURNIP GRATIN

Ingredients

- ½ yellow onion

- 1½ lbs turnip

- 1 garlic clove

- ½ cup fresh chives, finely chopped

- 2 oz butter

- 1¼ cups heavy whipping cream

- 7 oz shredded cheese

- ½ tsp salt

- ¼ tsp ground black pepper

Instructions

1. Preheat the oven to 200° C.

2. Peel the onion, garlic, and seasoning. Slice all very finely with a mandolin or food processor.

3. Chop the chives perfectly.

4. Grease a 9" baking dish with butter and add slices of onion, garlic and chives, and most cheese, save some on top— salt and pepper to taste.

5. Add cream and remaining cheese on top. Bake until bubbly and golden brown for about 30 min

Prep time: 15 min; **Servings:** 6

Macros: Net Carbs 8 % (8 g) Fiber 2 g Fat 81 % (35 g) Protein 11 % (11 g) 387

WHITE TURKEY CHILI

Ingredients

- 1 lb Organic ground turkey (or ground beef, lamb or pork)

- 2 cups riced cauliflower

- 2 cups full-fat coconut milk (or heavy cream)

- 2 Tbsp. coconut oil

- ½ a Vidalia onion

- 2 garlic cloves

- 1 Tbsp. mustard

- 1 tsp each: salt, black pepper, thyme, celery salt, garlic powder

Instructions

1. Heat the coconut oil in a large pan.

2. Saute garlic and onion. Stir in the ground turkey for 2-3 min.Break with the spatula and stir until it crumbles continuously.

3. Place cauliflower and rice in the seasoning mix and stir well.

4. Add the coconut milk once the meat is browned, bring it to a simmer and reduce for 5-8 minutes, stirring frequently. For an extra thick sauce, mix in shredded cheese.

Servings: 5; **Prep time:** 5 min

Macros: Cal 388   Fat 30.5g Carbs 5.5g Protein 28.8g

BALSAMIC ROASTED TURNIPS

Ingredients

- 3 turnips

- 2 Tbsp balsamic vinaigrette

- 1 Tbsp garlic

Instructions

1. Heat the oven to 400° F.

2. Peel and cut turnips into cubes.

3. Combine turnips, 2 Tbsp balsamic dressing, and garlic in a bowl.

4. Place the turnips on a parchment paper-lined baking sheet.

5. Bake for 30 min.

Prep time: 10 min, **Servings:** 3

Macros: Cal 32 Fat 0g Carbs Net Carbs 7g Fiber 3g Protein 1g

CRISPY KALE CHIPS

Ingredients

- 2 cups kale

- 2 Tbsp Himalayan sea salt

- Avocado oil spray

Instructions

1. Preheats oven to 350° F.

2. Cut the kale and spread it on a parchment paper-lined baking sheet.

3. Spray the avocado oil spray kale.

4. Coat with the Himalayan sea salt 2 Tbsp.

5. Bake 15-20 min or till it is crispy.

Prep time: 3min, **Servings:** 2

Macros: Fat 0g Carbs Net Carbs 3g Fiber 2g Protein 2g

CREAMY TURNIP KETO "MASHED POTATOES" WITH BACON

Ingredients

- 4 large turnips

- ½ cup bacon bits

- 2 Tbsp grass-fed butter

- ½ cup almond milk

Instructions

1. Peel, clean, and cut turnips into cubes.

2. Place in a saucepan and fill with water. Bring water to a boil and simmer until tender for 12-15 min

3. Strain and rinse cooked turnips.

4. Place in a large mixing bowl and break turnips into smaller bits using a fork.

5. Combine all the ingredients. Mix to the desired consistency.

Prep time:10min; **Servings:** 6

Macros: Fat 7g Carbs Net Carbs 3g Fiber 1g Protein 1g

CRISPY ROASTED EGGPLANT CHIPS

Ingredients

- ¼ cup olive oil

- 1 Large eggplant (thinly sliced)

- ½ tsp salt

- ¼ tsp pepper

- 1 tsp garlic powder

- ½ tsp dried basil

- ½ tsp dried oregano

- ¼ cup parmesan cheese

Instructions

1. Preheat the oven to 325° C.

2. Mix ¼ cup extra virgin olive oil and dried spices in a small bowl. Coat sliced eggplant. Set on a baking tray.

3. Bake until the chips are evenly browned for about 15-20 min. Flip over the baking time halfway through.

4. Remove from the oven and sprinkle with Parmesan cheese.

Prep time: 10 min; **Servings:** 15

Macros: Cal 60 Fat 5g Carbs Net Carbs 2g Protein 1g

KETO CABBAGE CASSEROLE

Ingredients

5. 2 lbs green cabbage

6. 1 yellow onion

7. 2 garlic cloves

8. 4 oz butter

9. 1½ cups heavy whipping cream

10. 6 Tbsp sour cream or crème fraîche

11. 6 oz cream cheese

12. 1 Tbsp ranch seasoning

13. ½ tsp ground black pepper

14. 1 tsp salt

15. 6 oz shredded cheese

Instructions

1. Preheat the oven to 200 ° C. Use a sharp knife or mandolin slicer to cut onion, garlic, and green cabbage.

2. Heat and add the butter to a large frying pan. Sauté the vegetables for about 8-10 minutes until softened. Remove milk, sour cream, cheese with butter and spices. Remove thoroughly and allow another 5–10 min to simmer.

3. Add to a baking dish. Sprinkle the cheese on top and bake until the cheese melts and turns golden for 20 min

Prep time: 15 min; **Servings:** 6

Macros: Net Carbs 7 % (11 g) Fiber 4 g Fat 84 % (57 g) Protein 8 % (13 g) 612

ROASTED CABBAGE

Ingredients

- 2 lbs green cabbage

- 6 oz butter

- 1 tsp salt

- ¼ tsp ground black pepper

Instructions

6. Preheat the oven to 200 ° C.

7. Melt the butter with medium-low heat in a casserole.

8. Divide the green cabbage into wedges and cut in the middle of the thick stem. Cut slices - less than 1 inch thick and place in a large baking dish or on a baking sheet lined with parchment paper.

9. Add pepper, salt, and pour over the melted butter.

10. Bake till the cabbage is roasted for 20 min

Prep time: 10 min; **Servings:** 4

Macros: Net Carbs 8 % (8 g) Fiber 6 g Fat 88 % (35 g) Protein 4 % (3 g) 365

KETO TORTILLAS

Ingredients

- 2 eggs

- 2 egg whites

- 5 oz cream cheese

- 1½ tsp ground psyllium husk powder

- 1 Tbsp coconut flour

- ½ tsp salt

Instructions

6. Preheat the oven to 200 ° C.

7. Beat the white eggs and bacon until smooth. Continue to beat, preferably for a few min, with a hand mixer. Add cream cheese and mix until a smooth batter.

8. In a small bowl, add oil, psyllium husk, and coconut flour. Add 1 spoonful of flour mixture to the butter and mix well. Let the batter sit for a couple of min, like a pancake batter,

until it gets thick. How fast the swelling of the mixture depends on psyllium husk powder brand— some trial and error may be required.

9. Take out 2 sheets of baking and put on each parchment paper. Using a spatula, distribute the batter thinly into 4–6 circles or 2 rectangles (not more than 1/4 inch thick).

10. Bake for about 5 min or more on the upper rack until the tortilla turns around the edges a little yellow. Carefully check the bottom side to prevent it from burning.

11. Serve with your choice oFilling. We love them with beef and salsa tex-mixed ground! So cheese is a winner all the time.

Prep time: 5 min, **Servings:** 6

Macros: Net Carbs 6 % (2 g) Fiber 1 g Fat 78 % (10 g) Protein 17 % (5 g) 116

KETO STUFFING

Ingredients

- 2 Tbsp butter

- 2 yellow onions, finely chopped

- 5 oz bacon, diced

- 8 oz celery root, diced

- 1 apple, grated

- 2 oz pecans, chopped

- 2 buns or slices of low-carb bread

- 1 cup heavy whipping cream

- 2 lbs ground pork

- fresh sage 2-3 sprigs, finely chopped

- ½ tsp ground nutmeg

- 1 tsp salt

- ½ tsp ground black pepper

- 1 Tbsp butter

Instruction

1. Preheat the oven to 175 ° C.

2. In oil, ghee, lard or duck fat, brown onions, bacon, and celery root until golden.

3. Stir in ⅔ sage (save the remainder for garnish), plus all the grated apple and pecans. Let it cool.

4. Crumble or split the low-carb bread slices in a large bowl and pour over the heavy cream.

5. Add the ground beef, spices, and the mixture of brown onion and garlic.

6. Put in a grated baking dish and bake for 25–30 min in the oven or until the meat is cooked thoroughly.

Prep time: 20 min; **Servings:** 8

Macros: Net Carbs 6 % (8 g) Fiber 2 g Fat 76 % (46 g) Protein 18 % (25 g) 543

PARMESAN-ROASTED GREEN BEANS

Ingredients

5. 1 egg

6. 2 Tbsp olive oil

7. 1 tsp onion powder

8. ½ tsp salt

9. ¼ tsp pepper

10. 1 lb fresh green beans

11. 1 oz parmesan cheese, grated

Instructions

5. Preheat to 200 ° C in the oven. Whisk together eggs, butter, and spices in a pan. Remove the beans and stir until the egg batter covers all the green beans.

6. Remove excess fluid and stir vigorously with parmesan cheese.

7. Place the beans on a parchment paper-lined baking sheet. Bake for 15–20 min at the upper level in the oven.

Prep time: 10 min; **Servings:** 4

CRANBERRY SAUCE

Ingredients

- 12 oz fresh cranberries

- Zest of a medium orange

- 1 tsp stevia

- ½ tsp vanilla extract

- 3/4 cup water

Instructions

1. In a pot, add all ingredients and bring to a boil.

2. Reduce heat and cook 15 min

Servings: 6; **Prep time:** 30 min

Macros: Cal 27 Fat 0.1g Carbs 7.2g (4.5g net) Protein 0.3g

BROWN BUTTER BUFFALO BITES

Ingredients

- 1 head of cauliflower (approx 3 cups oFlorets)

- ¼ cup hot sauce

- 2 Tbsp. Grass-Fed Butter

- 2 garlic cloves

- Pinch of salt

Instructions

1. Melt the butter and take it to low heat until browned.

2. At that time, but in florets, your cauliflower.

3. Add a big pan.

4. Preheat the oven to 400°F. Then add garlic to the butter, and it should be almost ready.

5. When browned, cut the butter and pour over the cauliflower. Add hot sauce.

6. To move the flowers to a sheet pan, use tongs. Set them up side by side. Save the remaining extra sauce in the pan.

7. Bake for 20 min.

Prep time: 10 min; **Servings:** 2

Macros: Cal 175 Fat 11g Carbs 10g Protein 4g

KETO CHICKEN HEMP HEART TENDERS

Ingredients

- 1 cup hemp hearts

- 1.5 lbs boneless skinless pastured chicken breast (2)

- 2 large eggs

- 1 Tbsp apple cider vinegar

- 2 Tbsp water

- 2 Tbsp garlic powder,

- 2 Tbsp flax meal

- 1 Tbsp nutritional yeast

- 1 tsp salt

Instructions

1. Preheat oven to 425 F.

2. Cut the chicken fillet into strips. Set aside.

3. Place hemp hearts in a saucepan.

4. Beat the egg, water, and vinegar in the second bowl.

5. Nutritional yeast, flax meal, garlic powder, and salt are combined in the fifth pan.

6. Grease the pan carefully.

7. Lightly cover each smoothie with the flax mixture, sprinkle the egg mixture, and cover it with the hemp core before placing it on the plate.

8. Bake 15 min Use a spatula to move things around for 15 min

9. Use a scraper to scrape the oven to prevent breadcrumbs from sticking to the tray. Use your favorite sauce to eat.

Prep time: 15 min

Macros: Cal 558 Fat 33.3g Carbs 7.4g Fiber 7g Protein 57.4g

CUCUMBER CAPRESE SALAD

Ingredients

- ½ cup cherry tomatoes

- 1 medium cucumber (roughly chopped)

- ½ cup mozzarella cheese, cubed

- 1 bunch basil (finely chopped)

- 1 small shallot (thinly sliced)

- 2 Tbsp olive oil

- 2 Tbsp balsamic vinegar

- 1 clove garlic (finely minced)

- ½ tsp salt

- ¼ tsp pepper

Instructions

1. Mix balsamic vinegar, olive oil, garlic, salt, and pepper in a bowl.

2. Add cucumbers, onions, cheese, shallots, and basil. Toss gently until well covered.

Prep time: 5 min; **Servings:** 2

Macros: Cal 112 Fat 10g Carbs Net Carbs 2g Protein 4g

GARLIC PARMESAN ZUCCHINI PASTA

Ingredients

8. 4 medium zucchini (spiralized into noodles)

9. 2 Tbsp extra virgin olive oil

10. 4 cloves garlic

11. ½ cup chopped tomatoes

12. ½ cup shredded Parmesan cheese

13. 1 cup fresh basil leaves

14. 2 tsp lemon juice

Instructions

6. Add olive oil, garlic, and red flakes of pepper in a skillet. When the oil begins to bubble with the garlic, add the zucchini's noodles. Throw the noodles and bake for 3-4 min Turn the water off.

7. Incorporate onions, basil, lemon juice, parmesan cheese. Toss to dress up.

8. Serve with the option of grilled chicken, steak, or shrimp.

9. Garnish with additional parmesan cheese.

Prep time: 5 min **Servings:** 4

Macros: Cal 83 Fat 7g Carbs 5g Fiber 2g Protein 1g

CREAMED SPINACH

Ingredients

- 4 cloves garlic, sliced

- 2 Tbsp ghee

- 1 lb raw baby spinach

- ½ tsp fine Himalayan salt

- Pinch of nutmeg

- ½ tsp black pepper

- 8 oz lactose-free cream cheese

Instructions

1. Place over medium heat a large skillet.

2. Add the garlic and ghee.

3. Add the spinach and cover with a lid for 2-3 min

4. Open the cover and stir well. Add salt, nutmeg, and pepper to taste.

5. Keep stirring until the spinach is dark green and release liquid once all the spinach is wilted.

6. Extract until the liquid evaporates, then blend until smooth and creamy in cream cheese.

Prep time: 5 min; **Servings:** 4

Macros: Cal 162 Fat 15g Carbs 5g Fiber 1g Protein 3g

JALAPEÑO PARMESAN CRISPS

Ingredients

- 1 large jalapeno

- ¼ tsp red pepper flakes

- A pinch of pink salt

- ½ tsp dried oregano

- ½ cup grated parmesan, separated

- ¼ cup finely shredded sharp cheddar

Instructions

6. Preheat the oven to 425 F and use parchment paper to line a baking sheet.

7. Slice jalapeño thinly. Bake 5 min. Remove from oven, set aside, and cool.

8. Whisk spices and parmesan together.

9. Pour 1 cup spice and a mixture of parmesan into piles and flatten into small circles.

10. Place jalapeño slices on top of the mixture of parmesan and spice. Sprinkle the cheddar cheese on top of the jalapeño.

11. Bake for 8 min

Prep time: 5 min; **Servings:** 10 to 12

Macros: Cal 30 Fat 2.3 Carbs 0.2 Protein 2.5

CELERIAC OVEN FRIES

Ingredients

- 1 large celeriac root

- 3 Tbsp. coconut oil

- 2 tsp Everything Bagel Seasoning

Instructions

1. Preheat oven to 400° F.

2. Cut off the celeriac's twisted roots and peel

3. Cut and cut into slices. Soak the fries in water for 20 min with a little lemon.

4. Drain, rinse, and season with coconut oil.

5. Spread and bake for 30 min on a sheet pan, then turn off the oven and let them sit for another 10 min

6. Open the oven; make a shake for the sheet pan.

Prep time: 30 min; **Servings:** 4

Macros: Cal 133 Fat 9.8 Carbs 9 Protein 1.5

NO POTATO SALAD

Ingredients

- 1 head Cauliflower

- ½ cup Keto-friendly mayo

- ¼ cup mustard

- 3 hard-boiled eggs

- 4 slices bacon, cooked

- 2 stalks celery, chopped

- 2–3 Tbsp dill

- 2–3 Tbsp green onions, chopped

- 1 tsp sea salt

- 1 tsp black pepper

- 1–2 Tbsp white wine vinegar

- 1 scoop Perfect Keto Unflavored Collagen

Instructions

1. Combine and set aside the collagen and mayo.

2. Mix all ingredients, including mayo and collagen, and use your hands to blend.

Prep time: 20 min; **Servings:** 4

Macros: Cal 415Fat 35.2gCarbs 9.8g (5.5g net)Fiber 4.3gProtein 25g

CREAMY KETO SPINACH ARTICHOKE DIP

Ingredients

- ½ cup mozzarella cheese (shredded)

- ½ cup parmesan (shredded)

- ¼ cup nutritional yeast

- 10 oz frozen spinach (thawed and drained)

- 12 oz artichoke hearts

- 2 cloves garlic (finely chopped)

- ¼ cup sour cream

- ½ cup cream cheese

- ¼ cup mayonnaise

- ½ tsp salt

- ¼ tsp pepper

- 1 tsp garlic powder

Instructions

1. Preheat the oven to 375 ° C.

2. Add all ingredients in a large bowl. Mix well until everything is well mixed. Pour in a glass pie bowl or shallow baking dish.

3. Bake for about 20-25 min

Prep time: 10 min; **Servings:** 2

Macros: Cal 139Fat 8g Carbs Net Carbs 5g

BRUSSELS SPROUTS WITH BACON

Ingredients

- 16 oz bacon

- 16 oz raw brussels sprouts

- Salt and Pepper

Instructions

1. Oven preheats to 400° F. Line a baking sheet with paper on the parchment.

2. Half the sprouts of Brussels.

3. Cut bacon lengthwise into small pieces using kitchen shears.

4. In a prepared baking sheet, add brussels sprouts and bacon and season with salt and pepper.

5. Bake for 35-40 min.

Servings: 6; **Prep time:** 10 min

Macros: Cal 113 Fat 6.9g Carbs 6.8g (3.9g net) Protein 7.9g

KETO STIR FRY WITH CABBAGE NOODLES

Ingredients

- 1 lb of pastured chicken breast

- 1 head of green cabbage

- 1 clove of garlic (chopped)

- ½ white onion (diced)

- 2 Tbsp extra virgin olive oil

Instructions

1. Heat Tbsp olive oil or wok over medium-high heat.

2. Add the chopped garlic and cook to a minute for 30 seconds.

3. Cook 5-7 min or until translucent, add diced onion.

4. Add the remaining olive oil and chicken breast (ground or chopped).

5. Stir fry until the chicken is crispy

6. Chop the head of cabbage into long strings like noodles.

7. Add cabbage amino, bell pepper, and coconut — season with freshly grated ginger, sea salt, and black pepper.

8. Saute until the cabbage is soft but crispy for 3-5 min

Prep time: 5 min; **Servings:** 4

Macros: Cal 251 Fat 14.8g Carbs 4.8g

BAKED KETO SPAGHETTI SQUASH

Ingredients

5. 1 spaghetti squash

6. 1 Tbsp olive oil

7. 1 tsp Himalayan sea salt

8. 1 tsp pepper

Instructions

1. Preheat the oven to 400° F.

2. Line a baking sheet with parchment paper.

3. Split the spaghetti squash either way down the middle

4. Drizzle the olive oil, salt, and pepper on the spaghetti squash

5. Place the spaghetti squash on the plate and put it in the oven for 40 min

Prep time: 5 min; **Servings:** 4

Macros: Cal 31 Fat 0.6g Carbs 7g (Net Carbs 5.5g) Protein 0.6g

GRILLED ASPARAGUS SALAD

Ingredients

- 1 scoop Perfect Keto Micro Greens Powder

- 1 handful of Italian parsley

- 3 Tbsp lemon juice

- 1 tsp lemon zest

- 4 Tbsp extra virgin olive oil

- 1 Tbsp monk fruit or stevia

- ¾ tsp salt

- ½ tsp black pepper

- 1 lb asparagus

Instructions

1. Heat a grill pan at medium-high heat or set the BBQ on fire.

2. With Tbsp olive oil, 1/4 tsp salt, and a pinch of pepper, drizzle asparagus spears.

3. Grill asparagus up to slightly charred and tender for 5-6 min

4. In the meantime, add Perfect keto greens to a high-speed blender by adding powder, parsley, lemon juice, lemon zest, olive oil, sweetener, and remaining salt and pepper. Mix up to smooth. Change to taste the seasoning.

5. Cut asparagus into 1 "bits and use vinaigrette to drizzle. Toss to dress up. Serve cold, hot, or room temperature in a large bowl.

Servings: 4; **Prep time:** 10min

Macros: Cal 76 Fat 7g Carbs 2g (1g net) Fiber 1g Protein 1g

KETO PIGS IN A BLANKET

Ingredients

- 4 medium hot dogs

- ½ cup shredded mozzarella cheese

- 3/4 cup Almond Flour

- 1 large Egg

- ¼ tsp Baking powder

- ¼ tsp garlic powder

- ½ tsp Pink Himalayan Salt

- ½ tsp Sesame Seeds

Instructions

1. Cut each hot dog into 3 pieces and set aside.

2. Melt the mozzarella in the microwave and add almond flour and egg. Mix well

3. Add baking powder, garlic, and salt. Mix well.

4. Divide dough into 12 pieces of the same size and roll the dough.

5. Put the balls of dough on a baking sheet covered with parchment. Press each ball into an oval shape.

6. Place each piece of hot dog in the dough and wrap it as if in a blanket.

7. Sprinkle with sesame seeds (press to adhere to the dough).

8. Bake in the oven at 350° for 17-20 min.

Servings: 4; **Prep time:** 10 min

Macros: Cal 332.25Cal from Fat 248 Fat 27.5g42% Carbs 7.25g2% Fiber 2.25g9% Protein 16.25g33%

AVOCADO & EGG FAT BOMBS OR DEVILED EGGS

Ingredients

- 3 large eggs

- ½ large avocado, peeled and without seeds (100 g)

- ¼ cup mayonnaise (55 g): you can do it yourself

- 1 Tbsp lemon juice or lime

- ½ tsp salt, or to taste

- freshly ground black pepper

- 2 Tbsp chopped chives or chives

Instructions

1. Boil the eggs. Fill a small pot of water 3-quarters full. Add a pinch of salt. When finished, remove from heat and place in a bowl of cold water. Remove the shells when the eggs are cool.

2. Cut the avocado in half and remove the seeds and peel them. Cut the eggs in half and carefully, without breaking the egg whites, place the yolks in a bowl.

3. Mix the avocado, egg yolks, mayonnaise, lemon juice, salt, and pepper.

4. Serve with slices of cucumber and sweet onion, or fill in protein halves and make deviled eggs.

Prep time: 10 min; **Servings:** 1

Macros: 1.1 gram of net carbs Protein 2.2 g Fat 14.8 g Cal148 Total Carbohydrate 2.5 g Fiber 1.4 g Sugar 0.3 g Saturated fat 2.7 g

CHEESY KETO CREAMED SPINACH

Ingredients

- 3 Tbsp butter

- 1 tsp onion powder

- 2 cloves garlic, minced

- 2 (10oz) packages frozen chopped spinach, thawed and drained or equivalent fresh

- 1 Tbsp butter

- 4 oz cream cheese

- 1 cup heavy cream

- ½ cup grated Parmesan.

- salt and pepper

Instructions

1. Fry the garlic and onion powder in 3 Tbsp butter. Mix the spinach and simmer for about 5 min

2. In another skillet, mix 1 Tbsp butter with cream cheese, heavy cream, and parmesan cheese. Cook over medium heat until cream cheese melts. Add salt and pepper to taste.

3. Add the cooked spinach cheese sauce.

Prep time: 25 min; **Servings:** 2

Macros: Cal 352| Carbs 2g | Protein 13g | Fat 28g | Saturated Fat 20g | Cholesterol 102mg | Sodium 658mg | Potassium 148mg | Sugar 1g | Vitamin A: 2100IU | Vitamin C: 4.1mg | Calcium: 390mg | Iron: 0.5mg

KETO PUMPKIN SPICE LATTE CUPCAKES

Ingredients

5. 64 g of almond flour

6. 15 g of golden flax flour

7. 9 g of psyllium skin

8. 1 ¼ tsp of baking powder

9. 1 tsp pumpkin pie with herbs

10. ¼ tsp xanthan gum

11. 2 tsp ground flaxseed

12. A pinch of kosher salt

13. 2 eggs

14. ½ cup gold alloyed

15. ⅓ cup erythritol gold xylitol

16. 1 tsp vanilla extract

17. 1 tsp apple cider vinegar

18. 1 Tbsp instant coffee beans

19. 42 g of unsalted butter

20. 60 g of golden cream and coconut acid + 2 tsp apple cider vinegar

- 21 g coconut flour

- 3/4 tsp pumpkin pie spice

- 1 Tbsp erythritol

- ¼ tsp kosher salt

- 33 g pecans

Instructions

1. Preheat the oven to 180° C.

2. Grease and dust a muffin pan with coconut flour.

3. Add almond flour, flax flour, psyllium husk, baking powder, pumpkin spice, xanthan gum, and salt in a medium bowl. Beat until homogeneous, reserve.

4. Add the sweetener and eggs in a large bowl and electric mixer for 3 to 5 min until it is airy and lighter in color. With the blender, add vanilla extract, apple cider vinegar, coffee, and butter.

5. Add the dry flour mixture in 2 parts, alternating with sour cream. Continue mixing for 2 min until it is completely absorbed and elastic (the dough thickens when you mix it!).

6. Place the dough on the prepared muffin pan, matching the back of a wet spoon. If you fill them with the pumpkin filling: spoon 3/4 full of dough, add a Tbsp pumpkin cream cheese and cover with a thin mixture. Sprinkle with almond streusel (if used).

7. Bake 23 to 27 min without filling and 30 to 35 min with filling. Let it cool in the pan for 15 min before removing it and let it cool completely on a rack if it has frosting.

Prep time: 20 min; **Servings:** 6

Macros: Cal 130 Fat 14g Saturated Fat 6g Carbs 4g Fiber 2g Protein 4g

KETO LOADED BROCCOLI CAULIFLOWER SALAD

Ingredients

- 1 cup mayonnaise

- 1 Tbsp Swerve or other sweetener

- 2 Tbsp apple cider vinegar

- 3 cups raw broccoli

- 3 cups fresh cauliflower

- ½ chopped red onion

- ½ cup grated cheddar cheese

- 8 g of cooked and grated bacon

- ½ cup natural walnut pieces

Instructions

1. Add the mayonnaise, the vinegar and the apple cider in a bowl. Beat to combine.

2. Mix vinaigrette and other ingredients well in a large bowl.

3. Cool until use.

Prep time: 10 min; **Servings:** 12

Macros: Cal 235

KETO ROLLS WITH SPINACH ARTICHOKE DIP

Ingredients:

Rolls:

- 6 g of cream cheese block

- 2 ¼ cups grated mozzarella cheese

- 3 large eggs

- 2 ¼ Tbsp non-aluminum baking powder

- 1 cup + ½ Tbsp almond flour

- red almond flour

Dip:

- 1 can (7 oz) artichoke hearts, drained and chopped

- ¼ cup sour cream

- 4 g of cream cheese

- ½ cup mozzarella

- ¼ cup parmesan

- 1 ½ cup fresh spinach, finely chopped

- 1 clove garlic minced

- ¼ tsp salt

- A pinch of pepper

- ¼ onion, thinly sliced

Instructions

- Preheat the oven to 400° F

- Melt the cream cheese and mozzarella in a small saucepan over low heat. It must be a thick, sticky paste. You can also use the microwave.

- Put the melted cheese with the baking powder, almond flour, and eggs in a large bowl. Mix until smooth and cold for 10-20 min Roll in 12 scoops and cool in the refrigerator for at least 10 min until ready.

- While the dough is cooling, savor the spinach, mix all the ingredients in a large bowl until they come together.

- Place the balls of dough around the edge of the pan by touching both sides. Fill the middle with spinach sauce. Bake for 17 to 20 min until the rolls are spongy, golden brown and well cooked. Serve.

Prep time: 30 min; **Servings:** 8

Macros: Cal 239 fat (g) 20.1 Carbs (g) 5 net carbs 3.8 protein (gram) 12.7 sugar (gram) 2.2

AVOCADO CAPRESE

Ingredients

- ½ cup grape tomatoes or cherry tomatoes, cut in half

- 120 g of mozzarella balls (bocconcini)

- 2 Tbsp homemade pesto or bought in store

- 1 tsp minced garlic

- ¼ cup olive oil

- Season with salt and pepper

- 2 ripe avocados, peeled, seeded and halved

- Fresh basil leaves to serve (optional)

- 2 Tbsp balsamic glaze reduction to drizzle

- 2 Tbsp chopped fresh basil

Instructions

4. Mix tomatoes, mozzarella balls, pesto, garlic, olive oil, salt, and pepper in a bowl. Mix well to combine all tastes evenly.

5. Place the prepared avocado halves on a plate with fresh basil leaves.

6. Pour Caprese in each avocado half and sprinkle with balsamic glaze. Garnish with chopped fresh basil.

Prep time: 15 min **Servings:** 4

Macros: Cal 341   Carbs 15 g|Protein 8g Fat 29 g Saturated Fat 7 g Cholesterol 22 mg Sodium 220 mg Potassium 550 mg Fiber 6 g Sugar 4g Calcium: 165 mg | Iron: 0.8 mg

SPAGHETTI SQUASH AU GRATIN

Ingredients

8. 1 medium-sized spaghetti squash

9. 1 lb chicken fillet

10. 1 medium onion, diced

11. 2 Tbsp butter

12. 2 grated garlic cloves

13. 3/4 cup Greek yogurt or sour cream

14. 1 ⅓ cup cheddar cheese

15. ½ tsp salt

16. ½ tsp black pepper

Instructions

4. Preheat the oven to 375 F.

5. Cut the pumpkin in half and scoop out the seeds. Season the spaghetti squash with a little olive oil, salt, and pepper.

6. Place the skin on a leaf drawer with a border covered with foil.

7. Cut the chicken fillet so that you have 4 pieces of chicken. Place the chicken in the pan, season with salt and pepper.

8. Bake for 45 min. When the pumpkin is cooked, scrape the meat with a fork to make noodles and cut the chicken into small pieces.

9. While the chicken and pumpkin are cooking, place the onions with the butter in a pan on the stove over medium heat until they are very soft.

10. When everything is cooked, combine the pumpkin noodles with spaghetti, chicken, onion, yogurt, 1 cup cheese, salt, and pepper in a large bowl.

11. Place the mixture again in the empty bowls and cover with the cheeses and place under the grill until golden brown.

Prep time: 15 min;

Macros: Cal 295 Carbs 14 g Protein 26g Fat 15 g Saturated Fat 8 g Cholesterol 86 mg Sodium 508 mg | Potassium 539 mg Fiber 3g Sugar 6g Vitamin A: 586IU Vitamin C: 6 mg Calcium: 255 mg Iron: 1 mg

STUFFED MUSHROOMS WITH HAM AND CHEESE

Ingredients

- 8 large white mushrooms

- 3 oz soft cream cheese

- 1 ½ cups of grated cheese

- 1 ½ cups minced ham

- 1 tsp garlic salt

Instructions

6. Preheat the oven to 400° F.

7. Remove the mushroom stalks and throw them away or save them for another use. Mix all other ingredients.

8. Bake for 30 min or until the mushrooms soften and the filling is golden brown.

Prep time: 10 min; Servings: 6

Macros: Total Fat 12g18% |Saturated Fat 6g| 30% Cholesterol 44mg15%| Sodium 770mg32%| Potassium 286mg8%| Total Carbs 2g1% | Dietary Fiber 0g0%| Sugar 1g| Protein 12g24% Vitamin A5.7%| Vitamin C1.4%| Calcium12%| Iron3.6%|

KETO ZUCCHINI CINNAMON APPLES

Ingredients

- 2-3 medium zucchini, peeled and seeded

- ¼ cup butter

- ½ cup low-carb sugar substitute

- ½ tsp Sukrin Fiber Syrup Gold

- 1 Tbsp lemon juice

- 1 ½ tsp apple extract or vanilla extract

- 1 tsp cinnamon

Instructions

1. Slice zucchini into apple-like slices.

2. Heat butter in skillet. Add zucchini slices and cook until tender.

3. Mix remaining ingredients and add to zucchini. Sprinkle in xanthan or guar gum as needed to thicken — Cook and stir about 5 more min

Prep time: 20 min; **Servings:** 4

Macros: Cal 92 Carbs 3g |Protein 1g Fat 9g | Saturated Fat 6g Cholesterol 24mg Sodium 78mg | Potassium 157mg Fiber 1g |Sugar 1g Vitamin A: 450°IU Vitamin C: 14.9mg Calcium: 20mg | Iron: 0.2mg

KALE SALAD WITH GOAT CHEESE AND POMEGRANATE

Ingredients

● 12 oz kale

● 2 Tbsp olive oil

● ½ tsp salt

● ½ cup pumpkin seeds

● ½ pomegranate, peeled and seeds separated

- 8 oz goat cheese or feta cheese

- vinaigrette

- ½ cup olive oil

- 2 Tbsp balsamic vinegar

- 1 Tbsp Dijon mustard

- 3 Tbsp orange juice

- sea salt and ground black pepper

Instructions

1. Cut the ribs/stems of each bare leaf. Cut the peel into small pieces. Place on a plate or large bowl.

2. To soften baldness, sprinkle with a pinch of salt and spray with olive oil and massage the baldness with your hands until it becomes dark.

3. Roast pumpkin seeds in a dry skillet over medium heat until they have a little color. Set aside.

4. Wash the pomegranate.

5. Beat all the ingredients in the vinaigrette in a bowl. Pour it over the peeled and mix.

6. Add almost all the pumpkin and pomegranate seeds, keep to decorate, and mix.

7. Crumble the cheese on the salad and cover with remaining pomegranate and pumpkin seeds — season with freshly ground black pepper and sea salt.

Prep time: 25 min; **Servings:** 1

Macros: Net Carbs 8% (7 g) Fiber 3 g Fat 79% (29 g) Protein 13% (11 g) 331

LEBANESE GARLIC CREAM

Ingredients

- 2 cloves garlic

- 2 Tbsp lemon juice

- ½ tsp salt

- 2 Protein

- 1 cup light olive oil

- ½ tsp sumac (optional)

Instructions

1. Add crushed garlic, lemon juice, salt, and egg whites in a large, narrow cup or cup.

2. Use a hand blender to mix until fluffy; It takes about 1 minute.

3. Put the oil in a thin stream while continuing to mix. The garlic cream is ready when it is thick, white, and fluffy. Cover with a little sumac or chili powder.

Servings: 1; **Prep time:** 10 min

Macro: Net Carbs 1% (1 g) Fiber 0 g Fat 98% (54 g) Protein 2% (2 g) 490

GRILLED MANCHEGO HAM AND CHEESE SALAD

Ingredients

- 1 big head of lettuce

- 1 cup olive oil, divided

- 3 oz prosciutto

- 3 oz manchego cheese

- ½ lemon juice

- 1 pinch of salt

- 1 pinch of ground black pepper

Instructions

1. Preheat grill for 20 min over low heat.

2. Cut the lettuce in half. Brush the inside with olive oil. Place the lettuce upside down on the grill and roast with the limb open for a few minutes on each side. After turning, brush gently with a little more olive oil. Roast until outer leaves are lightly crisped.

3. Shave Manchego cheese with a peeler or cutting blade or grater. Cut the ham into small pieces.

4. Mix the lettuce in a deep bowl with the rest of the olive oil. Sprinkle with lemon juice, season with salt and pepper. Mix to combine.

5. Cover with layered chips and pieces of ham.

missing info

CONCLUSION

We have come to the end of this beautiful journey through the best seasonings, light and simple that have delighted you with your favorite dishes.

Keep cooking and preparing them to accompany all the dishes you prefer.

They are great and very easy to prepare.

I thank you for accompanying me on this journey and I embrace you, see you at the next recipes.

Lightning Source UK Ltd.
Milton Keynes UK
UKHW020827190421
382245UK00011B/598

9 781667 165332